Healing Encounters in the City

Insights from an urban perspective

by

Martin Wallace

Vicar, St. Marks, Forest Gate; Priest in Charge, Emmanuel, Forest Gate; Area Dean of Newham

with a Foreword

by

Jim Thompson

Bishop of Stepney

GROVE BOOKS LIMITED

Bramcote   Nottingham   NG9 3DS

CONTENTS

Page

Foreword by Jim Thompson, Bishop of Stepney   3

Introduction.   4

1   Discovering God's Healing Today.   6

2.   Healing in the Community.   8

3.   Healing in the Individual   12

4.   Varieties of Healing   16

5.   Healing Within   20

6.   Summary.   23

ACKNOWLEDGMENTS

My thanks go to the many people in the parishes in which I have worked, for without them my personal journey into healing could never have taken place. I am also indebted to Jean Petersen and Diana Reed who struggled valiantly to decipher my scribble and turn it into a typed manuscript. This book is dedicated to my wife Diana whom God used to introduce me to the healing ministry, and whose love, patience, and encouragement in that ministry is something I value beyond words.

Martin Wallace

THE COVER PICTURE

is by Peter Ashton

First Impression February 1987

ISSN 0144–171X

ISBN 1 85176 046 5

FOREWORD

It has often been said that parish-based theology is the glory of the Church of England. This book describes a personal journey of a parish priest. It contains those precious insights which come from the mixture of Bible study, prayer, down-to-earth pastoral care and a vision inspired by Christ. It is very far from the popular press stereotype of a trendy, woolly-minded vicar. The theology has been formed in the crucible of a dedicated love of God and service of people.

The healing ministry of the Church has often been seen as a fringe activity, to be regarded with suspicion and caution. But slowly and surely the proper healing ministry of Christ has begun to be expressed and lived out within the ordinary main-line ministry of the Church.

Sometimes there seems such an enormous gap between the miraculous times of the New Testament and our own sceptical age. Many people have suspended belief and listened to Jesus' healing miracles as though they were at best a pious exaggeration, and at worst a legend. Yet we live in an age which is full of its own amazing miracles which would have made the New Testament generation gasp in astonishment. The laser operating on the eye, trans-continental television, space travel and the microchip are part of our real world, and yet we find it difficult to believe that the God of all creation should, through his Son, be able to give the blind their sight and enable crippled limbs to be healed. Martin Wallace builds bridges between that age and ours, and enables us to see the quiet miracles as belonging to our own time.

The great word 'shalom' is used to evoke that wholesome, life-giving, healing peace of God which comes from the power and the presence of God among us. Shalom is profoundly God's wish for his earth, and this does not just apply to individuals who suffer and need healing, but also to the community and the environment which are damaged and hurt by social inequality and injustice. Martin does not let us off the hook by saying that the healing ministry to which the Church is called is just an individual matter, but rightly moves on to say that we have a care for the whole society, which in itself is in desperate need of the healing shalom of God.

Many Christians who will have seen and experienced and prayed for the healing power of the Spirit will be encouraged and strengthened by this important reminder of the greatest healing resource of all, namely the love of Christ.

Bishop Jim Thompson of Stepney

INTRODUCTION

Books on Christian healing are published by the score these days—so why one more? Many books on healing are helpful and good, but, as one who has read a number of them, I observe that many of these books appear either to be packed with academic theology, or to recount the success story of one particular ministry, or to attempt to tell the Christian Church 'how to heal' in twelve easy lessons! The end-result can be that what we read actually takes away what little confidence we already had. And so many appear to have the theory of healing worked out in such a way that the Spirit is no longer given the freedom 'to blow where he wills' (see John 3.8). Of course, this is a caricature of the situation, but what these few pages aim to do is to show that the healing Spirit of God is far broader than any tight doctrine we may construct, and that our theology of Christian healing is derived from a constant interaction between both our experience and our Biblical understanding. One way to present the case for such an interaction is by the use of anecdote together with some discourse—the method chosen by the Gospel writers to present their theologies of Jesus' ministry. So what follows is personal and Biblically reflective. Its aim is to encourage the reader to explore the Christian healing ministry, despite any fears that might otherwise inhibit.

The Bible is essentially the story of God's relationship with his creation, from before Time to the Second Coming and beyond. The most powerful presentation of Jesus we have has been handed down in the form of stories—and from these stories we are left to draw all sorts of conclusions about the nature of Jesus, his work and his message. Particular episodes in the life of Jesus, and particular remarks he made, must be interpreted in the context of the whole of his life-story. And his life-story must be interpreted within the context of the whole of God's story, as we have received it. We may know of dreadful conclusions reached by those who isolate the evidence and use gospel stories and proof-texts out of context to support a particular view. For example, Mark 5.1-20, the story of Legion, has been used to show that all mental illness is really demonic possession. In the same way, we may know of destructive conclusions reached about healing by those who generalize from a very small number of experiences and come out with statements like 'God always heals people', or 'You have not been healed because you have unresolved moral failure in your life!' The wholesale damage done to people from such statements is surely an offence to God himself. Similarly, there is often amazing 'double-think' from some Christians: a Christian who decides at work to build luxury flats on inner-city dockland area because the profit yield will be high, can hardly pray with clean hands for those whose health suffers through living in damp and draughty slums.

The whole subject of Christian healing thus concerns very much more than just healing services, and there is a great deal we cannot understand simply because God and his work are not reducible to formulae the human brain can tackle. Indeed, my own travelling into the healing ministry increasingly convinces me that any 'completed' theology of healing, however attractive, is always deficient. I find I construct a theology to encompass all my experiences and reflections, only to discover something new happens which falls outside my neat theory. So I construct a new theology to include that fresh observation, only to discover a fresh insight which falls beyond even that new theory, and so it goes on. The Kingdom of God is a bigger city than we can ever hope to explore fully.

But this is nothing new: far from giving us a neatly packaged theology of Jesus' healing miracles, the Evangelists themselves evidently found it difficult or undesirable to do so. They present us with accounts of various examples of healing and use different words to describe them. This variety of words is important, for it gives us a clue about the breadth of the healing ministry and the limited vision we impose on ourselves by using just the word 'healing' to cover such a multitude of events.

Sometimes a healing will be described as *ergon,* a work of God (John 9.1-12), where his creating skill is witnessed. Or it may be seen as a cure, *iaomai,* (Luke 14.4), restoring people's health. It may be a wonder, *terata,* giving rise to a sense of awe for all around, and a sign, *semeion,* pointing people's attention to God (both John 4.48). Jesus describes his healing work as therapy, *therapeuo* (Luke 5.31), easing people into a balanced state of well-being. At other times the theme is power, *dunamis,* (Mark 5.30), where the dynamite of God's love is seen to explode the apparently solid rock of disease. Another facet is revealed in the use of the word *ekballo* (Mark 1.39) in the context of casting out demons.

Each evangelist has his own favourites (often John uses 'sign' and Mark uses 'power', for example), and maybe each was culturally conditioned to use particular words. But the fact remains that the Evangelists use a plethora of descriptions for an activity we tend to reduce to the common word 'healing'. This verbal reductionism must not lead us into theological reductionism. Indeed, it is this very rich variety of Biblical material that must form the backcloth to our exploration of healing to-day.

The Spirit blows where he wills, and we as Christians need to learn again how to be led by the Spirit rather than attempt to put him into a straitjacket for our own convenience. It is unnerving and often awesome, but always exhilarating, refreshing and surprising. These pages, then, are anecdotal—an account of a journey observing and following the Spirit of God in a very faltering way, often groping in the dark, Bible in hand, to wherever he leads. Certainly we can learn from others also on this journey, but no-one else can make the journey for us. We may feel that emotionally or intellectually we identify, perhaps, with the cynicism of the Bishop of Durham about miracles, perhaps with the exciting ministry of John Wimber, or any stage in between. But in the end, the journey has to be our own, taking as few preconceptions as possible, and being ready to admit that the Holy Spirit, not we, is in charge of the journey.

1. DISCOVERING GOD'S HEALING TO-DAY

As a child, I was brought up to believe that miracles may or may not have happened in Biblical times, but certainly not to-day. At church each week we prayed for a long list of sick people, none of whom I knew personally. If a name was omitted from this list, I never knew whether it was because that person had recovered, died, or been forgotten!

Then while my wife was expecting our first child she developed osteo-arthritis in her feet. It became so bad she could not walk fifty yards, and the consultant agreed to operate. After months of waiting for a hospital bed, in frustration I prayed one night simply that she might get better. That week we walked five miles, the operation was cancelled, and that was thirteen years ago now. My experience and observation forced my theology to change to accommodate this event. A powerful work of God had happened without a doubt. Diana's feet were restored by God's activity alone and it was as dramatic as the healing of the paralyzed man in Mark 2.1-12.

A couple of years later, a Christian woman asked for prayer for the trouble she was experiencing with her spine: traction and collars appeared not to be helping. We prayed and nothing dramatic seemed to happen except that in the ensuing months I experienced occasional back pains in the same place as she did, and during that time she completely recovered! I have wondered since if there is a contact here with the story of Jesus healing the woman with the issue of blood (Luke 8.42-48)—Jesus knew from something happening within him that someone else was being healed. It began to dawn on me that the details of the stories of healing miracles in the Gospels as well as the general fact of these events are important and have lessons to teach us to-day. Prayer for healing may be personally draining—if it was so even for Jesus, why not for us too?

Following these two incidents I began occasional healing services on a weekday evening, not wanting to force this focus onto the main congregation. There was no wide publicity, but soon after moving them to Sunday evenings developments made us bring them to a halt. Firstly, people from other churches began to appear, suggesting God was more present or active at one church than another, whereas Jesus healed all over the place, not just in one or two 'spiritual' centres. Indeed, in talking with the Samaritan woman (John 4.21-24) Jesus suggests 'holy places' are obsolete. Secondly, people were coming to these services rather than others, suggesting some services were more 'healing' than others. However, all worship must be concerned with the healing of our souls, minds and our bodies, and Holy Communion is *the* service celebrating the greatest healing of all between God and his creation. Such services are now held about twice a year simply to serve as a focus, while at any other service, laying on of hands can be requested—either at the Communion rail during the administration, or during the intercessions at other services.

At healing services, lay people are always involved in the ministry, following the example of Jesus commissioning the 12 and the 72, often with one person sitting at the back for those too shy to come to the front, perhaps like the woman with the issue of blood who tried nervously to hide in the crowd around Jesus? Not everyone can or should cope with the gaze of the public!

The lay people who minister are usually women, so that an alternative ministry to that from male clergy is offered: for example, a woman with a gynaecological problem may well feel more relaxed explaining that to another woman.

The congregation can never hear the conversation or prayers between the one ministering and the one requesting, but they are encouraged to watch, and in their imaginations lift those they see into God's care, relaxed in the knowledge that he knows the details and that is all that matters. Thus it is a ministry for the whole congregation, with those laying on hands being merely the visual symbols and channels for the healing gifts given through the whole Body (1 Cor. 12). There are no 'star healers'.

During these services, some are helped, some declare they are healed soon afterwards, but we have never witnessed an instant healing, and let us be honest, for some nothing seems to happen at all. What has been fascinating to observe, however, is how the congregation as a whole has become a more united and 'healed' group over the years, these services having been an important part in that. There is no frenzied emotion. Quiet music is usually played in the background, often people quietly cry, and always there is a sense of release and peace as emotional honesty is allowed. Indeed, it may well be the peace that attracts people to be present even if they do not wish to come forward for prayer. Certainly, 'healing peace' is in short supply in our world (and often in our church life!) and healing must always be about *shalom*—wholeness, healthy, unity, peace, and God's loving rule in our lives . . . not an anaemic feeling of passivity, but a dynamic sensation of being at one with each other and with God as we determine to live and work in and for the Kingdom.

2. HEALING IN THE COMMUNITY

None of our Christian ministry can ever happen in a vacuum. People do not become ill without a reason—a germ, virus, accident, stress, or environmental pollution. Our individual state of health is related to the wider world in which we live, and so our ministry of individual healing must be set in a wider context too. There is a vital perspective that must be included in our understanding of the healing ministry.

In recent years there has been a welcome converging of those Christians intent on a 'spiritual and personal' ministry and those intent on proclaiming a 'social gospel'. So private prayers for healing and public work for justice no longer appear as alternatives, but as complementary. It is interesting that these are held together in the vision given to John of life in Heaven, in Revelation. God's *shalom* certainly includes a corporate as well as an individual peace.

In Revelation 22.1-5 we are presented with a vision of Heaven—an experience of God and his Kingdom in which everything and everyone is whole and good and free from decay. This is God's Kingdom in its fullness—that same Kingdom that comes upon individuals who are healed by the love of Jesus. In fact our personal healing in this life is only a tiny foretaste of the grand and total healing to be experienced in Heaven. This is *shalom* in its corporate and total entirety.

When I walk the streets of East London in the Borough of Newham I see much that is good and happy and buoyant. Many of the people have a healthy zest for life and an ability to look adversity in the face. West Ham football fans sing 'I'm forever blowing bubbles', and it is this ability to 'blow bubbles' at difficulty that is part of the East End's character. But I also see a picture that appears like a photographic negative of that vision of Heaven. In Revelation, John sees the Father on the throne with Jesus, acknowledged and worshipped. But in reality here I see God is most certainly not enthroned by 90% of the population—without wishing to make too much of Anglican church attendance in the Borough of Newham, with a population of over 200,000, I note that only about 1,000 are in our churches on a Sunday. Of course, there are many other Christian groups meeting, but the Anglican figures are one indicator. Many simply cannot 'see' God at all. I recall the man I visited, who saw church like school—'stand up when teacher enters, sit when told, get your books out, be told off, then go!' He was not prepared to relive an experience of autocratic authority and failure. Then there is the man who came to church one Sunday evening recounting his recent appearance in court; every time he mentioned the magistrate he pointed to the sanctuary—he could only relate to God as an unanswerable judge. There are those working in huge factories where the situation conjures up memories of Bosch's pictures of Hell rather than John's vision of Heaven, and where they have become accustomed to seeing themselves as cogs in an impersonal universe.

Revelation speaks of the clear water of his Spirit flowing freely through the street, but outside my door dirty water flows into (and out of!) ancient sewers crumbling beneath the road. Instead of Heaven's tree of life and leaves for the healing of the nations, the trees are few in number, vandalized, and surrounded with canine deposits. Different nations do not discover healing, but rather the various ethnic groups find racism, distrust, victimization and discrimination at school, in the police station, at work and when shopping, and so the energetic ones do battle with each other verbally, culturally and physically. The street, the school, and the youth club are all venues for division, antagonism and anger. In Heaven, we are told, nothing is under God's curse. But much that *is* 'under God's curse' is found in the city in the form of personal selfishness (lying to climb the enormous housing list), greed (sale of stolen goods), immorality (prostitution and drug peddling), in the form of institutionalized crime (rate-capping the most deprived Boroughs), and social deprivation.

The London Borough of Newham is classified by the Department of the Environment as the second most deprived Borough in the entire country. The 1981 census figures (now hopelessly out of date) revealed *then* individual parishes in Newham were suffering 22% unemployment, 14% overcrowding (nationally 3%), 14% single parent households (nationally 5%), households lacking basic amenities 25% (nationally 4%), 53% ethnic minorities (nationally 4%), 31% unskilled workers (nationally 18%); add to that 107 tower blocks with more people living above the tenth floor than anywhere else in the country, the second highest level of households with no bath, the highest percentage of children in poor housing and from low socio-economic groups, less than 1% with professional qualifications, over 27,000 receiving supplementary benefit, only 8% of young people entering higher education (31% in Richmond-upon-Thames), the lowest rate of library book borrowing in London, massive violence and crime rates—and the list could go on. All this is squeezed into nearly a quarter of a million people living in an area just four miles square. It is therefore hardly surprising that the mortality rate is 15% higher than for the country as a whole, and the perinatal mortality rate a staggering 55% higher! The relationship between deprivation and health can hardly be seen more clearly. If you also consider poor wages, insecure jobs, powerlessness, pollution, noise, few leisure amenities, it is obviously absurd to be a church ministering purely individual healing while the environment is causing so many casualties.

Unlike John's vision of Heaven, we do not not see free worship from easily identified believers, but rather Christians who admit their faith often in the face of hostile abuse from their peers, and active discrimination by their employers. At a selection panel for head teachers it was stated by one official that as one candidate was a church-warden he would automatically be unsuitable in a multi-ethnic school!

Unlike Heaven, where there is 'no night', the darkness is long and a good deal of shadowy activity goes on in the office where business deals are clinched, in the factory where time-sheets are fiddled, in the home where children are abused, and in the club where drugs are pushed. God's throne is not seen in the city and there is no clear picture of a wise and just use of power and responsibility. Vast crowds live and work in conditions that cause dis-ease, disease and disability of mind and body, and make it impossible for their souls to 'lift my eyes to the hills from whence comes my help' (Psalm 121). We are told that all sorts of physical, emotional and nervous problems can be directly encouraged by poor environment and diet. And again, all this can be shown by government statistics and graphs to be far worse in urban priority areas.

Of course the Church will continue to minister to individual cases of need. But as well as tending those who need the first aid, having fallen from the cliff, we also need to erect fences at the top to prevent further casualties. Counselling can reduce emotional anxiety, children's upbringing can be improved with increased resources, and feeding habits can be changed for the better through health education and financial help—it costs money to buy good food! Utopia will never arrive of course, and even in a Garden of Eden people will rebel and fall and need healing, but it is surely inescapable that prevention and cure go hand in hand. They are both to do with the Kingdom of God. So when Jesus lashed the Pharisees with his tongue because they devalued ordinary people (Matthew 23), upturned the traders' stalls in the Temple because they practised racial discrimination in degrading the Court of the Gentiles (Mark 11.15-19), commented on taxation which had been imposed by an alien authority (Mark 12.13-17) and spoke harsh words to the young man because of his selfishly hoarded riches (Matthew 19.16-22), he was working for healing just as much as when he tenderly approached Jairus' daughter (Mark 5.21-43).

Jesus entered the home of Zacchaeus. But it was not until Zacchaeus had recognized his responsibility to the poor that it was declared that salvation had come to him (Luke 19.1-10). As Christians we must be wary about benefiting from private health care either as a patient (the consequence of which can be that those who are ill *and* economically poor have to wait even longer for attention) or as practitioner (the motive for which can be to serve only those who can pay), if all we do is 'pray' for the poor who are sick. When Jesus quoted the Old Testament in the synagogue at Nazareth, almost using it as his 'manifesto' (Luke 4.15-21), that passage combined a reference to the poor, a note of hope to those imprisoned, a declaration of intent to restore physical sight, to work to free the oppressed, and to verbalize the Good News. From there Jesus went out and immediately began healing individuals. The concern for justice and corporate healing was not divorced from a concern from personal healing. The Kingdon of God has both an individuality and a communallity about it.

Of course, we would all acknowledge that the problem is so huge that many of us hardly know where to begin. Perhaps we start by discovering the facts about our local community, and then getting involved in tenants' associations, political parties, playgroups, women's groups, anti-racist projects, community care schemes, trade unions and environmental groups. It will mean those Christians with power in industry, commerce and the public sector will relate their faith to their work to ensure that decisions are made not just on the basis of profitability, but only after considering how far decision will further the encouragement of or disintegration of local people's *shalom,* i.e. the siting of a factory, the building of homes, the nature of leisure facilities, the resources for education. The work of the London Docklands Development Corporation is an obvious example of how private enterprise is pouring literally billions of' pounds into the Thames-side area of Newham, clearly with no local mandate, clearly with no intention of doing anything to alleviate Newham's deprivation, and clearly solely to serve the already affluent and create more profit for them. The Church's role in working for healing must include speaking out against this sort of injustice which is the very cause of personal illness, as well as ministering with prayer in homes and churches to those who are the sick casualties of a system that allows profit to overshadow justice.

Much of what has been described here is individual in example to Newham. Elsewhere the details will vary and the response may be seen in different terms. That is for each Christian to work out as God leads on. What may be helpful, however, is for us *all* to begin by asking how John's vision of Heaven in Revelation matches an observation of our own corner of God's world and the part we are playing in it.

3. HEALING IN THE INDIVIDUAL

One contribution of the Gospel stories is that we can relate to them because they are about are about people—and human nature does not change. It is as we consider these stories in the light of our contemporary observations that we are preserved from flying into a spiritual schizophrenia in which our Christian thinking and claims differ wildly from the reality of our lives.

The three brief meditations that follow are very simple skeletons designed to show how we can work at earthing our scriptural reading.

Mark 2.1-12: The healing of the man lowered through the roof
We do not know how long the man had been ill, nor do we know his emotions. But if he was normal he would have feelings of depression, anger and frustration at having to be dependent on others. Maybe he resented the crowd who had made it impossible for him to be near Jesus. Certainly he had to admit publicly that he was a sinner—that much is implicit (v.5: 'Your sins are forgiven'). We do not know whether his sins involved greed, pride, jealousy or other problems. I find a parallel in an experience with Christopher, whose pain from disintegrating inter-vertebral discs was healed only after an admission of hostile feelings towards his family and a willingness to repent. It was almost as if the 'weight' of guilt on his shoulders was removed, thus releasing the pressure on his spine. Perhaps we see a paralysis of guilt being dealt with by Jesus both 2,000 years ago and to-day? The Kingdom of God is surely about banishing both the causes and the effects of guilt!

The paralyzed man was fortunate to have friends to bring him to Jesus, for without them he would have remained paralyzed. So was Barry, who refused to come forward for healing of his stutter at a healing service, but was taken later to a different church and almost dragged to the front, where his speech was restored through public ministry of healing. Without his friends, his speech would still be impaired—teamwork, tim-ing and invitation are all vital, for the Kingdom is about mutual unselfishness.

The paralyzed man could not get to Jesus because those who were keen to learn from him gathered in such a way that they excluded the very one with the most need. This can be a picture of Christians at a healing ser-vice—so keen to see miracles that personal sensitivity for those in need is lost. I recall watching a dreadful scene at a church in which the minister turned the spotlight onto a child with crutches, with earnest encouraging sighs, groans and 'alleluias' from members of the congregation—and then told the poor distressed family to go home in faith and expectancy. I suspect it is precisely this insensitivity that scares people away from genuine encounter with God.

What about the householder whose roof was apparently destroyed in this Gospel story? Having Jesus in our home is one thing, but giving our home to him is another. It hardly needs stating that to open one's home so that Christian ministry can happen within it is to face the possiblity of urine on chairs, defaced wallpaper, damaged household items and theft. The miracle story holds true to life at this point too, and many ministers and others could tell a colourful tale!

The Scribes were also at hand, waiting to dismiss the event, just as to-day we often find the very people of God who should be rejoicing at healing, waiting to criticize and analyze. Maybe they are bound by fear, poor training, poverty of experience or deficient theology. Certainly this has been my observation of fellow Christians only too often. Perhaps healing will often cause conflict precisely because the Holy Spirit is the disturber, and when his power is seen in action then everyone has their true colours revealed.

John 5.1-18: The man at the pool

This man was presumably waiting for an angel to disturb the water, for the first one into the pool then would be healed—so ran the legend. How often to-day do we discover desperate people willing to clutch at any superstition or tradition ranging from lucky charms to faith healing, fringe medicine to Christian healing. Edith was convinced her house was haunt-ed and came for help laden with good luck charms, having already tried the spiritualists, Roman Catholics, Pentecostalists, doctor, social ser-vices and faith healers. At the pool Jesus did not collude with the man's superstition but clearly focused the man's attention on his own healing love and power. Similarly, Christians to-day face comparable situations and must react as Jesus did, making it clear that we are not para-medics nor twentieth century witch-doctors, but people who are willing to direct attention to the living Christ.

Jesus knew, (apparently without being told), the lame man had been ill for 38 years. Increasingly, I find the most releasing prayers are not those full of detail and diagnosis but those which focus on Jesus and his pre-ceding understanding and care. As stated earlier, at healing services our people are encouraged to imagine those receiving ministry simply sitting with Jesus or being touched by him, and are encouraged just to let him do the rest.

Jesus chose only one man in the crowd for healing. Why did he not heal the entire crowd? Why, to-day, is it true that not everyone is healed, even after specific prayer? Results often seem to bear little relationship to faith, expectancy, feeling, conviction, moral standing or anything else. The supremacy really does belong to the Lord. Our faith is not in method or style or even in prayer—but in Jesus. There are no trite answers. Alice was not healed of her multiple sclerosis when I was convinced she would be! But Nigel was healed of a paralyzed shoulder after prayers which I immediately forgot and even failed to enquire about later on! Rules hardly seem to apply!

Jesus then asked the man 'Do you want to be healed?'. On the face of it, a crazy question, and yet fundamental. Eric was an alcoholic whose marriage was in ruins and who asked for help in desperation. He assured me he had disposed of all drink in the house. We prayed, and I heard later that immediately I had left him he went and drank from his hidden bottle. He found it easier to hide from domestic responsibility than face up to it. Ron, on the other hand, was an alcoholic who after prayer became a new man in every sense of the word, ready to put a new energy into a helpful life. The man Jesus faced at the pool also had to be ready to work and take responsibility rather than just sit and beg. The question 'Do you want to be healed?' is just as important to-day. Belonging to the Kingdom involves moving on to a new life with new responsibilities.

Jesus then simply spoke to the man: there was no frenzy or great emotional appeal. His authority was self-evident. Recently, when Carol asked for prayer for her arthritic knee, I simply prayed quietly and calmly for a minute or two and her pain left her. The Gospels do not seem to suggest the need for shouting and heightened drama on the part of the minister.

When the Pharisees questioned the man, he could say very little about Jesus. Jesus set no pre-conditions and made no demands. Healing was a free gift offered without strings. We cannot say that this was true of all Jesus' healing miracles, for this clearly is not so—the Centurion's servant is healed only after a declaration and testing of faith (Matthew 8.5-13). Obviously each one is different, but Dolly came once to a healing service and was healed of an arthritic elbow even though I never saw her again. Jesus is obviously not in the business of only giving his gifts to those who acknowledge him or pass some test of faith! His healing, like the sunshine, is there for any who will enjoy it. The gates of the Kingdom are wide open, never shut (Revelation 21.25), and people are free to belong or not to belong. It is not a prison for unwilling victims. Some may use the Kingdom like a holiday health-spa and God seems to allow that.

Acts 3.1-10: The lame man at the Gate Beautiful
Here we are presented with a man who had, presumably, often been passed by the worshippers at the Temple. He sat at the Temple gate because religious people are often seen as, at best, generous, and at worst, a soft touch. I guess that they had often thrown coins into his begging bowl, for that is what he wanted from Pewter and John. But by giving cash, they would have been helping the man *in* his disability, not *out* of it. Our healing ministry is not about sustaining dependence, but rather about helping people to discover a new sense of self-responsibility. In my own ministry Beatrice seemed to hang on every word I said following a healing God gave her. That dependence was unhealthy and she then needed to be healed of that through careful and loving distancing. It reminds us of the way Jesus had to tell the healed man 'Legion' not to follow him but to return home (Mark 5.18-19).

The worshippers may have passed the man regularly, and that is an image that may speak to our consciences. No doubt we all pass others on the way to our church gatherings, unaware of their needs or unable to see how to make the love of Jesus relevant. What is more, these same worshippers were amazed when the man was actually healed! Again, our honesty urges us to admit that sometimes we attend worship with little expectancy that God will act. I recall Ted telling the congregation how God had healed his piles some weeks earlier! The sharp intakes of breath that ran through the people is something I shall never forget!

The lame man, then, had already received much will-intentioned help, and there is much good in giving, welfare and social work. But in the end our ministry is diminished if it does not also reveal the distinctive power of God. I have a feeling that many look to other cults and sects for religious experience precisely because so often the traditional churches are hesitant in naming our Lord publicly. Here, Peter and John were involved in a caring church community (Acts 6.1-6), but they went further and offered the personal and miraculous love of Jesus. It reminds me of Kim, who felt lonely, abused and unloved. She was brought to church to 'make friends', following an overdose. But it was not just her emotional and mental state that was helped: her soul was healed too as she met Jesus and experienced him as a new and real friend. Like the lame man, she expected one thing but found another.

It must have taken great courage for peter to have taken this public step of faith. Despite the previous chapter's record that 'many miracles' were being done, this is the first recorded public miracle in which he was involved. He must have realized how stupid he would have looked if nothing happened! But in any area of ministry we have to begin somewhere. The first healing service I ever conducted was something of a disappointment in that nothing tangible seemed to happen except that a few faithful friends said they 'felt good'. All our steps in the healing ministry are taken slowly and hesitantly, and are often full of anxiety. Sometimes we are bound to look stupid—'the fool for Christ'. Sometimes people will be disappointed. No-one taught or trained me in this ministry, and during four years at theological college we had just one lecture on healing. I make many mistakes, and suspect I am not alone. But sometimes we have to step out in faith, and rely not on technique, experience or ourselves, but on God. We need to be more concerned with loving faithfulness than egocentric success.

We read in the story that Peter ordered the man to walk in the name of Jesus Christ. If I am honest, I have only ever 'ordered in the name of Jesus' where I felt there was demonic possession. If I am to be true to scripture then perhaps I need to accept that sometimes conversational prayer with God is not enough for healing—that there needs to be a confrontation with the dis-ease in the name of Jesus. There is much I still need to learn. God's educational programme is never over for any of us.

At the end of this passage we are told that the man left 'walking and jumping and praising God'—he found new joy in an abandoned expression of worship expressed through his healed body. Sometimes prayer for healing does end that way: Catherine became a Christian after she was healed of acute depression and would tell everyone and anyone. On the other hand, four-year-old Tricia was healed of serious colon problems, but her parents soon seemed to forget God was responsible for their daughter's new health. Nevertheless, the aim in all our healing ministry will always be the same—ultimately to give glory to God himself.

4. VARIETIES OF HEALING

In practice, Christian ministry rarely begins by sitting comfortably in an armchair by the fire and attempting to discover how, by starting with Scripture, we can go out to do the same in Jesus' name. Much ministry is reactive, and it is only during or after the event we can even begin to make any sense of it in a Christian way. Both the event in which we are involved, and our attitude, need to be placed in a Biblical perspective. If this is not done and our ministry is not earthed in Scripture, we run the risk of creating a theological system measured against nothing but our own small experience. In the examples which follow, space and propriety dictate that only the barest details are given.

So how might we experience the personal healing of the Kingdom?

A. Expectations
(1) Tom lived with his difficult wife, and I took communion to him each month. He was housebound because of impaired balance through damage to his inner ear. As he explained the problem, I realized that if Jesus was physically present, he would simply reach out and heal him. To my shame, my own courage failed and I did nothing but imagine the scene. There were no expectations, little faith, no verbal prayers, and yet from that day he was physically 'cured'. Jesus claimed that 'curing' was part of his healing ministry, as on the occasion when he healed the man on the Sabbath (Luke 14.4). Tom was cured by the living Jesus too.

(2) James, on the other hand, was a young lad with a problem needing a series of operations. His family asked for prayer and after lengthy discussion we prayed simply, and all felt full of emotion and hope. 'Does that mean I don't need more operations?' he asked. How should you answer a five-year-old? The sad fact is that operations have followed and will continue to follow for James. Nagging doubts remain about the wisdom of praying with children and with parents whose emotions and faith can be raised and dashed so easily. Faith, love and expectancy were all present, but not only has no 'cure' been forthcoming, but rather things were made even more difficult for a time.

For both Tom and James, we must allow that the Spirit blows where he will—and there is much we do not understand. On a human level, the two experiences seem irreconcilable and yet they both happened and we need to admit that, rather than attempt mental gymnastics in trying to find a tight theology that explains both. We must accept the facts of reality as Jesus had to—the rich young ruler left Jesus with his life unhealed (Matthew 19.16-30), some others were not touched by physical healing (Mark 6.5). What is surely unfounded from both observation and from Scripture is that people are *always* healed or *never* healed by God. We simply have to be ready for both possibilities.

B. Prayer
(1) Deborah was admitted to hospital with cancer. As a Christian she had never revealed a very personal faith and after I prayed I left her.

Later that week the hospital chaplain visited her at my request, anointed her with oil (James 5.13-14), and she became a new person, not physically but spiritually. She was not *cured*—but she died *healed:* Deborah entered Heaven certain that death was not to be feared, and left behind an intensely moving testimony of personal peace and faith. It was a wonder to behold for everyone who knew her, and in its way just as awe-inspiring as the miracles described as 'signs and wonders' in John's Gospel. We were all left wanting to do nothing other than give praise to an amazing Lord who affects people at their deepest levels.

(2)   Joan and Peter's marriage was childless, and a destructive bitterness had entered in. Praying and counselling were rewarded by God not only with a strong marriage and a lovely baby, but also with both of them becoming Christians. When Jesus healed ten lepers (Luke 17.11-19) the one thankful leper is told he has been *saved*—perhaps saved from his disease and also from spiritual death. It was similar with Joan and Peter.

C. Healing Services
(1)   Colin came forward asking for prayers for his wife, who was desperately ill in hospital. The one ministering the laying on of hands that evening prayed for his wife only after praying for Colin that his own anxieties and concerns might be laid to rest. Not only did his wife cover but Colin himself left in good health. In Luke 5.31 Jesus describes his ministry to some Pharisees as 'putting people in good health', a state of being which encompasses our bodies, emotions, minds, relationships etc., and that is how it was with Colin. Jesus is in the business of setting a new equilibrium with life, not necessarily just putting the clock back on physical decay.

(2)   When Anne came forward asking for healing for arthritis in her hands, there was little emotion or awareness of special faith. But in the middle of that night she awoke, opening and closing her fingers quickly, giggling with delight! God had given a dramatic and powerful healing which is exactly how Luke the physician describes the healings of Jesus (Luke 5.17).

D. Orthodox Medicine
(1)   Alan was due to have a hip replacement and was very frightened. He asked for prayer for healing so that the operation could be avoided. After counselling we prayed that God would heal through whatever means he intended—medical or spiritual—recognizing that all healing properties are given by God. In the event, Alan agreed to the operation but then died in the operating theatre. My head knew all the right answers, but my heart was full of guilt at having encouraged him to undergo the operation, for not having prepared him for death, and for apparently having partly colluded with him that Christian healing could be an avoidance of pain. I knew that as a Christian his death was total healing and brought to him the offer of a new body. But it was a reminder that the ministry of healing treads a path full of questions and pain as it must have done for

17

Jesus—some could not be healed (Mark 6.5-6), some rejected his advice (Mark 7.36) and some were ready only to criticize (Mark 2.6-7). The healing ministry can be a minefield!

(2)   On the other hand, Freda and John had been under medical supervision from some time, receiving help for infertility. They asked for prayer, desperate for a child. With real feelings of uncertainty we prayed for them, only to be delighted six weeks later with the news of a pregnancy. Like the woman who had spent all her money on doctors, only to be disappointed (Mark 5.25), but then to discover Jesus could heal her, so Freda and John found healing outside the medical profession's expertise. For everyone, a sign had been given which pointed to the life-giving graciousness of God. In John 4.52 the healing of the official's son is seen as an indisputable sign for all the world to see and use in their search for a real and living God. Freda and John's baby also was an indisputable sign from God and towards God.

E. Bereavement
(1)   Douglas confided that he had refused to call a doctor even when he knew his wife was dying. Racked with guilt, afraid of the law, he was convinced he had committed murder and so excluded himself from God's love and from the gates of Heaven. As we were together the cloud seemed to lift and the counselling and praying became an informal confessional with absolution. He was restored—it was healing therapy, which is how Matthew often describes Jesus' healing miracles (e.g. Matthew 8.16) and we do well to remember that ministry through calm caring is as much a healing as the powerful and dramatic experience.

(2)   Elaine's husband had died some weeks earlier and she had insisted on keeping his ashes at home. Soon she was claiming to see visions of her husband, to notice objects move, and to experience various 'mists and smells'. Removing the ashes and counselling her to accept that her husband had died was the therapy, again, through which she received healing. It was not exorcism and this instance.

F. Deliverance
(1)   But with the Smith family it was different. Their pregnant daughter, Karen, staying with them, was losing weight. She claimed to be possessed by her dead father. As I entered the room she curled into a ball in the corner. It transpired that her mother had been to a spiritualist. Each time I prayed for the girl to be freed in Jesus' name she vomited physically. It was extremely unnerving and very frightening. We arranged for her to be admitted to hosptial and I advised that she should return to her own home, away from the spiritualistic environment in which she was presently staying. There was happy co-operation between the Christian minister continuing the deliverance ministry of Jesus (e.g. Mark 1.39), and the local medical staff; Karen gave birth to a lovely baby some weeks

later and has had no further trouble of that nature. It is surely undeniable that for Jesus deliverance was a real part of healing, and it would therefore seem likely that it should be a part of our contemporary healing ministry as the Church, the Body of Christ, continues his work.

(2)   Sarah had moved into her flat and in clearing out the cellar disturbed some old items. She became frightened, the dog became unsettled and so did the baby. Not being convinced this was genuine supernatural activity, I prayed briefly for peace for those who entered each room as we moved about the house, and we removed the offending items from her cellar into my dustbin. I also prayed for Sarah herself, shat she might know not only the removal of evil but the positive presence of Jesus. The problems in the home immediately ceased and Sarah professed conversion soon after. It would be lovely to end there, but honesty reveals that her new faith was short-lived, although her peace has remained. As with so many of Jesus' miracles, it seems that often he gives healing without conditions of personal commitment. For example, of the ten lepers cured (Luke 17.11-18) nine seemed to make no attempt to respond personally to the love of Jesus. Love by its very nature can hardly demand returns!

No two experiences of healing are the same: each one is a unique gift. That was true in Jesus' ministry in Palestine—hence the variety of words and descriptions used in the Gospels—and it is true to-day. What is also true—and so obvious it often seems forgotten—is that any understanding of healing that we have needs to be able to begin with the material of observation and experience with real peole and then be subjected to reflection in the light of Scripture. As we do that, we realize that, every time we venture falteringly with a prayer, the Spirit of God really is as free as the wind, which so often we 'do not know where it comes from or where it is going' (John 3.8).

5. HEALING WITHIN

Christian ministers can be the last ones to accept God's ministry for themselves either through other people or direct from God himself. As someone who had ministered and prayed with hundreds of people in their need, I have found being on the receiving end an invaluable learning experience. So again, this reflects the struggle to relate a Biblical failth with personal experience. For me, it centres upon the word *shalom*—that multi-faceted wholeness, peace and health God longs for us to enjoy, and which can come to us through any means he chooses. Shalom is not the anaemic experience of 'lack of trouble' usually rendered 'peace'. For the Hebrew it was profound, deep and all-encompassing: a state of balance and prosperity that is anything but static and negative. It embraces the warm security of living in harmonious community, the totally integrated personal life of body, heart and mind all attuned to nature, God and others, and also the justice, dignity and freedom in which everyone has 'enough'. The Shalom of God, then, 'which passes all understanding' is to do with his desire for total wellbeing. Again, in bringing his healing, his Shalom, the Spirit blows where he wills . . .

I had often wondered how my family and my congregation would cope if I was suddenly to be put out of action. The question became real when I suffered a crushed vertebra from a simple accident in the garden.

When I was taken into the ambulance, to my utter amazement the attendant who sat with me in the back of the vehicle was a member of his local church. God gave me a very real peace of mind—*shalom*—I realized that through a member of his Body, the Lord was with me even in an ambulance. Of all the ambulance men in our local authority, I wonder how many are Christians? Not many, I suspect.

Once in hospital, despite excellent nursing care, I found the first few days really dreadful. Whether it was a result of the pain or the drugs I do not know, but the most terrible depression fell over me like a heavy blanket. It was impossible to 'feel' God, utter even the most simplistic prayers or cope with a short Bible reading. I was also afraid for the future. What family would want a father who could not bend or sit? What church would want a vicar who could not lift even the lightest box? If my job was threatened, as a vicar so was my home. In later conversations it was interesting to realize just how totally unacceptable some people found this fact—that the vicar should be so depressed and anxious. It led me to consider what really were the expectations of the congregation and how did they normally perceive me? How important it is that the minister of a healing ministry does not try to suggest that he is infallible and not in need of healing himself! But again, God had all this in hand and wanted me to know his *shalom* . . .

In the weeks beforehand I had read two paperbacks, the first *Fearfully and Wonderfully Made,* in which Dr. Paul Brand and Philip Yancey detail their awe at the wonder of the human body which God has created. Their chapter on the skeleton was fixed in my mind: they focus attention on the natural healing properties of the body and contrast it with man-made structures—a broken bone will create new bone to cement a fracture in a way that a broken bridge can never of itself create new concrete to secure its own repair. As I remembered that chapter I began to realize that God was already very present in my body, working to heal the crushed bone with the natural properties he had implanted before I was even born.

The other book *Living with Jesus To-day,* by Juan Carlos Ortiz, spells out the age-old truth that as temples of the Holy Spirit then we do not need to go anywhere to meet with God: he is already very present deep within our bodies. As these two truths from the books fused in my mind, it dawned on me that of course God was in the hospital and was being very active, not least within my own body: He was closer than any Bible, prayer, or religious feeling. That day his gift to me was *shalom* of Spirit.

One question remains, however. Literally scores of Christians came to visit me, but why did only a very small handful offer to pray by my bed-side? How I longed for the offer of a quiet word of prayer. Was it embarrassment, or the feeling that 'it is the vicars who do the praying', or was it just plain spiritual inadequacy? Was it a reflection on my own public example and teaching? Did I inhibit public prayer? I did not necessarily want heroic prayers for dramatic healing, just quiet assur-ances of God's love. I wondered why the prayers that I knew were being uttered in private and at church meetings could not surface publicly with me in the ward. Perhaps a personal lesson for me must be to be more positive in offering a short and simple prayer with those who are laid aside, as an example as much as anything else.

Another lesson in bedside technique concerns humour. It was totally infuriating when visitors, probably out of a fear of having nothing much else to say, joked about my accident (I fell from a swing!). I had no way to answer, and from my perspective it certainly was no joking matter! But when I have been hospital visiting I know that often I have made jokes in similar ways, and I now notice the same glazed expression on patients' faces that I must have exhibited!

By the end of the first week I felt so much better that I decided to make myself useful. I appointed myself unofficial ward chaplain and resolved the next day to do a round of the beds. Why is it that clergy so often can only justify their existence by being active? God, however, had other ideas, knowing that if healing was to take place, then complete immobilization would be necessary. He was obviously concerned to give me *shalom* of body.

Most patients knew who I was by now from the streams of visitors both in and out of visiting hours, including a Bishop, an Archdeacon, and hordes of clergy. But the next morning when I was about to set off, my body was seized with the most terrible pain! God was confining me to bed in the only way possible! But God also knew my thirst to share his love. That day two nurses came and sat by my bed, and we talked about their faith (one a Hindu) and the worries they had relating their moral beliefs to some of the things they were asked to do as nurses. Then a doctor appeared and began to talk of her struggle to establish a Christian Union within the hospital. But loveliest of all was the patient awaiting a painful test, who had looked at the soap dispenser above her sink and at the symbol of two washing hands on it. She had recalled Dürer's famous drawing of praying hands and asked me to pray with her. God could even arrange events for me so that I could know his *shalom* in my conscience, worried by inactivity.

After a fortnight I was allowed home, still strapped up and with strict orders to remain horizontal on a hard bed. Every day for weeks there was a steady stream of visitors and cards. It was exhausting but humbling to be on the receiving end of so much care, especially as it included parishioners who were not members of the congregation. What was curious, however, was the way different people reacted to the sight of their vicar lying on his back, three feet below them.

For some it was plainly unacceptable: 'Get better soon, we need you as our shepherd'. 'I don't like seeing you down there when you are normally up in the pulpit'. These and other remarks revealed much about dependency, expectations, and public images. But for others, the effect was salutary. Some with whom I had never easily related before began to open up and expose their own vulnerability with a now very obviously vulnerable pastor. The *shalom* of the Body of Christ was being experienced and given by God in a deeper way than before. Above all, it was those very early visits that were the most valuable. Whenever I made hospital visits I had tended to leave the new patient for a few days to settle in before calling. I shall now try to do just the opposite. It is the first day or two in hospital—and then the initial days home again—when one needs the assurance of familiar faces or friends and family for comfort.

Ten weeks out of action is bound to cause some anxiety, at least on the part of this busy inner-city vicar! But how the congregation blossomed! Humour about not needing the vicar abounded (and relieved me). Parish life continued with just the occasional directive from my bedside, and what a joy it was to see the whole church operating even more fully than usual as the Body of Christ. God was giving them a new *shalom* in ministry.

Six months later, although by now I was back doing 90% of my normal duties, my back was still giving real pain and demanding a time lying down, because of inflamed and crushed inter-vertebral discs. Still I could hardly bend. How I fantasized about a hot Radox soak!

At Christmas, along with a card, we sent a duplicated letter giving our news, a fair bit of it this time spotlighting all that happened from my accident. We knew that many we sent to were Christians who walked closely with God. The amazing experience is that from that Christmas all my pain suddenly and totally disappeared. Without making extravagant claims, or having any idea what the future might hold, I know that God is still concerned to give me his perfect *shalom*.

All of this is very obviously a highly personal story, during which new insights about God's love and power in healing came about as a result of an unhappy experience, followed by a time of reflecting on how God is concerned. God's concern for the 'whole' of me cannot again ever be mere theory. It is as the theory is forged in the heated furnace of life that growth happens, which is surely true in all aspects of the healing ministry.

6. SUMMARY

The wind of God's Spirit blows, bringing peace and love, life and whole-ness, renewal and joy. This wind cannot be caught. Wind encased in a box ceases to be wind when it is forced to be still. Similarly, the Spirit of God cannot be contained by our limited understanding or experience. All we can do is to hoist our sails and be blown by Him, using Scripture to check our constantly changing position. Here and there we still need to tack as we discover rocks of danger, false expectations and disappoint-ment under us. Sometimes we will founder. Sometimes we will experience great exhilaration and excitement as we discover new horizons and see real examples of Christian healing.

For many of us, experience of healing will not be a daily occurrence. The examples in this book are drawn from a period of fifteen years in three very different parishes. There have been many unfulfilled hopes and many mistakes. The editing of stories has been selective. In the same way, the Acts of the Apostles covers about thirty years, and although it reads like an exhausting race through exciting days, there must surely have been many unrecorded times of frustration, mistakes and apparent-ly unanswered prayers. We must not assume we are going to get it right always. What we do need to discover is the confidence to go with God. Our confidence is based on him, not on a system of theology, a particular method, the example of a Christian leader, or on ourselves! We proceed ready to see what God will do in each new situation. What both Scripture and experience urge us to do is travel that journey of faith with him. And that journey will involve, amongst other things:

(1) a commitment not to reduce and limit the varieties of Christian healing

(2) an honesty about our personal theology changing with experience

(3) a determination to work at the social and preventive aspects of the healing ministry

(4) a readiness to read Scripture with our contemporary experience in mind

(5) an ability to set our observation of God's activity within a Biblical framework

(6) a willingness to interpret our personal lives with reference to God

Our understanding of God's healing love can never be static. It flows like a river between the bank of Scripture and the bank of experience. The nature of these banks determines the direction of the river of our understanding, which we can never predetermine. Our ministry may include seeing arthritis cured, a conscience calmed, a marriage recon-ciled, a racial tension eased, a housing programme enabled, a new faith experienced or a wanted baby conceived. Whenever these things happen we catch glimpses of the Kingdom of God. There is no equality in the brightness of light that each gives out to the world, and there is no blueprint that can be transferred easily from one situation to another. There is no single tight system of theology that can encompass all the evidence and all the answers. What we do have are encouragements to launch out with realistic faith in the name of Jesus.